Grief Looked Like Me

A Daughter's Journey Through the Loss of Both Parents

Minnina M. Smith

Contribution to Chapter 3

by

LaShon S. Smith

ISBN: 9798305479423

DEDICATION

To My Mother, Father, and Siblings

You were my first teachers, protectors, friends, and guides. Through your love, I learned the meaning of family, the importance of faith, and the resilience of the human spirit. Mom and Dad, though you are no longer with me in body, your love, care, and sacrifices live on through your children. This book is a tribute to your memory, and to the love and lessons you instilled in us—lessons that will continue to guide me throughout life. To my siblings, thank you for always being there, no matter the distance. Through life's ups and downs, we stand together. I love you all so much!

To Other Family Members We've Lost,

To both sets of grandparents, aunts and uncles. This is also dedicated to you. I was blessed to experience your care, love, good cooking, correction and humor. The journey through grief is not just about loss, but about the love and connections that remain even after we say goodbye. Thank you for the memories, the laughter, the tears, and the moments that shaped my world. This book is dedicated to the impact you had on my life, and for the eternal place you all will always hold in my heart.

To My Two Unborn Children

Though you were not born into this world, you will always hold a special place in my heart. I carry you with me in spirit every day, knowing that your souls are in heaven, watched over and at peace. While we never had the chance to meet, I will forever remember you. You are a part of me, and though your time here was brief within my body, your presence has left a lasting impact on my heart. You are loved, and I will always cherish the thought of what might have been, knowing that one day we will be together again.

CONTENTS

Introduction

Grief is something we all face at some point in life. It's an experience that knows no boundaries—whether it's the loss of a loved one, a relationship, or even a part of ourselves, the journey through grief can be overwhelming, isolating, and, at times, unbearable.

Grief Looked Like Me is my personal story, an attempt to put into words the complex emotions I've faced through significant losses—the loss of my mother, my father, and the grief that has shadowed me throughout life.

I've also included a special contribution from my sister, LaShon, who graciously shared her own experience of grief during the loss of our mother. Her perspective offers another layer to our shared journey through heartache, loss, and healing.

This book isn't just about the pain of loss; it's about what comes after. It's about healing—messy, unpredictable, and nonlinear healing. I wish I could tell you there's a clear roadmap, that you'll reach a point where you've 'graduated' from grief and it's over.

But the truth is, grief doesn't work that way. It ebbs and

flows. It shows up when you least expect it. And while the pain may soften over time, it never fully disappears.

My intention in writing Grief Looked Like Me is to offer a hand to those who are navigating their own grief journeys. If you've ever felt lost in your mourning, felt like no one truly understands, or felt as though you should be "over it" by now—this book is for you.

I hope that in sharing my story, you find comfort in knowing you're not alone. Healing is possible, and while it's not easy, it is worth the effort.

Thank you for joining me on this journey. I hope my words resonate with you and help bring you some peace, comfort, and perhaps even hope as you navigate your own path through grief.

1 THE LIGHT THAT WAS MY MOTHER

My mother and I shared a deep connection. She wasn't just my mother—she was the light in our family, the steady presence that kept us all grounded. Before cancer came, before we knew what losing her would truly mean, there was a woman full of life, strength, laughter and love.

There are four of us—each with our own unique bond to her. My sister, the oldest, was the trailblazer. She's the smart one, always leading the way for us. She graduated from college and earned her degree, setting an example we all admired. With her outgoing personality and a heart full of love, she's also a wonderful mother to five amazing children, four beautiful girls and one amazing boy.

I'm the second oldest, with no children of my own just yet—unless you count my beloved fur babies. I would call myself a creative spirit, a dreamer and a doer, unafraid to take on any challenge that comes my way, curious about the wonders of this life. I see possibilities everywhere, always looking for ways to make them reality.

Then there's James, the adventurer. He's the type who carves out his own path, never one to follow the crowd. He joined the Army at a young age, where he gained valuable experience. Now, as an entrepreneur and father to his beautiful daughter, he's determined to build something of his own.

Lastly, there's our youngest brother, Leonard. Quiet and reserved, he's the one who speaks volumes when you get him talking. He's the genius behind a computer, always fascinated by technology and the way things work. He may be soft-spoken, but he loves good food and conversation once you draw him out.

Each of us had our own unique bond with Mom, and that truly speaks to the kind of person she was. She had an incredible gift for connecting with each of us in a way that made our relationship with her feel deeply personal and special.

She had this remarkable ability to make us all feel loved and seen in our own individual way. Together, Mom, Dad, and us kids made up the fabric of our family, each of us shaped by their influence in different but meaningful ways.

Come take a walk down memory lane with me—back to the time when I was still a child, before cancer changed everything. I can still picture her—her laughter, her warmth, the way she made our house feel like home. She was more than a mother; she was the heart of our family.

I remember how she cared for us, the love she infused into everything she did. She was hardworking and simply an amazing mom. Those early years, especially before I turned 16, were filled with unforgettable moments. Long before breast cancer became part of our lives, she had already shaped us in ways I'm still uncovering today.

Let me take you back to some of the most beautiful memories about my mother. Not only was she beautiful, inside and out but she was kind, graceful, funny, silly, bold and when it came down to her children she did not play about us.

She had a way of balancing everything so seamlessly, at least it seemed that way to me. Even when things weren't perfect, she made it feel like they were. When it was time to be serious, we knew she meant business, but she also knew how to live, laugh, and have fun. She made life feel full in a way only she could. I admired her strength and resilience, not just as my mother, but as a woman.

I remember one time when we got caught in a flood. The waters were rising quickly, and we had to evacuate the car immediately. Somehow, my mom managed to drive the car near an auto body shop where some men were standing outside. I'll never forget how she got the three of us—me and my two brothers—out of the car, carrying one in front of her, balancing one on her hip, and the other on her back.

She waded through knee-high waters to meet the man who helped us reach higher, drier ground. She was truly amazing. Our home was always clean—except for the occasional mess in our bedrooms—cozy, and beautifully decorated.

It was filled with the wonderful smells of meals, most cooked from scratch, many of which were dishes she grew up with. She was always trying new things in the kitchen—sweet and sour meatballs, burrito casserole, fried fish, stuffed cabbage, fresh bread, and homemade soups, just to name a few. She didn't do too much baking of sweet foods but when she did bake, oh, her chocolate chip cookies, rolls and sweet potato pies were unmatched.

Mom is the reason I'm such a foodie today. With both her and my dad being such great cooks, it's a little surprising none of us ended up as chefs! But food was so much more than just a meal—it was a way for us to gather, to connect, to celebrate. Especially around the holidays…Let me tell you, my mom could throw down in the kitchen. Around Thanksgiving and Christmas, one of my all-time favorite dishes was her cornbread dressing (and if you don't know what that is, Google it, lol).

But seriously, cornbread dressing was more than just a side dish in our house—it was an entire experience, my hands down favorite. For me, it could've been the whole meal, and I wouldn't have needed anything else. Just cornbread dressing (not stuffing!) and some jellied cranberry sauce. Now, let me be clear—it has to be the kind without the whole berries and from the can. That whole berry stuff? No, thank you.

Mom would prepare a feast, and between her and my dad, there was always something new and delicious being made. Every now and then, she would whip up these yeast rolls *from scratch*—yes, from scratch!

The aroma would fill the entire house, and it was impossible to resist sneaking a piece or two before they were fully done. When they came out of the oven, fresh and hot, with butter melting on top? Pure heaven. Just thinking about it makes me hungry. Sometimes, she'd give us a tester or hand one over once they were ready, but I'll admit, I'd often sneak another when she wasn't looking.

During the holidays, we'd all gather around the table, everything perfectly set with nice glasses and plates, making it feel like a special occasion. I remember it being such a joyful time—the whole family together, eating until we were stuffed, laughing, and talking about everything under the sun. When we'd finally start to wind down, we'd either move to the living room or stay at the table, depending on how messy we were, especially as kids.

Then came dessert—maybe pie or cake—enjoyed with milk or hot cocoa. Those moments are ones I hold dear, memories I'll cherish forever. They were filled with warmth and love, wrapped up in the comfort of family and the best food you could imagine.

There's so much to say about her—so much more than just being my mom. Before she was a wife and a mother, she was a bright light in this world, a woman with a spirit that drew people in. To know her was to love her; she had that magnetic way about her.

Our mother's name was Carmen Carole Butler, born on June 14, 1950, in Milwaukee, Wisconsin, to Minnie Young and KC Butler. But before she became the matriarch of our family, Carmen was a young woman with dreams, ambitions, and a story all her own.

My mother's childhood shaped her into the fierce, loving woman we knew. From the schools she attended to the boyfriends she may have had, from the adventures she went on to the causes she fought for during the Civil Rights Movement, and her deep sense of justice and passion for life—she was so much more than just my mom. She had her own battles to fight, her own journey to navigate before we, her children, came into this world.

She endured hardships no one should have to face. But she was Carmen, affectionately known by her family as Carol or Cal—a woman who lived with purpose and determination, always striving to make her world better.

This is a picture of my mother in her youth, standing in the front, with my aunt behind her during a protest against segregation in the 60s.

Let me share a little more about who she truly was. From the schools she attended to how she was raised, the struggles she faced, and the dreams she had for who she wanted to become in this life—my mother's story is rich with layers.

She wasn't just my mom; she was a woman navigating her way through a world that wasn't always kind or fair to her. Her journey through life shaped her into someone deeply committed to justice, the treatment of others and during the civil rights movement, she stood up for what she believed in.

I believe Carmen Carol Butler had a strong sense of self and purpose, a drive to fight for what was right, and a passion for making a difference in the world around her.

Since I, nor my siblings of course, weren't around—nor even a thought in our mother's mind—when she was growing up, I found myself wanting to know more about her, not just as my mother, but as the little girl, the young woman before marriage and children. What were her goals and dreams? What did she ultimately want to do in life? To fill in the pieces of her story, I've made countless calls to my aunts and uncles, and I still do to this day.

My dear aunts and uncles from both sides of the family (my mother had four sisters and two brothers) have been my guiding lights in bringing her childhood and young adult years to life for me. Their memories and stories have added so much depth and love to the picture of who my mother was long before I came along, and they've been invaluable in inspiring me to write this book and in keeping her memory alive.

I will forever be grateful for the many conversations they graciously allowed me to have with each one of them.

2 THE DAY EVERYTHING CHANGED

I can still remember the moment as if it were yesterday. While some details are a little blurry due to the overwhelming emotional impact, the memory remains vivid.

About a year after moving to Fayetteville, NC, my mother's illness began to worsen significantly, impacting her physical strength and ability to do even the most basic things. She reached a point where she could no longer drive and had to rely on a wheelchair to move from one place to another.

Her condition was taking her down a frightening, uncertain path, and it became clear just how serious things were getting. Hospice started visiting our home, and with each visit, the reality of her situation hit harder. She had lost all her hair and so much weight, and she was too weak to stand on her own. Even the simplest tasks—grooming, bathing, everything—required assistance.

I often helped her with these tasks, though she didn't want the boys to see her in that condition. I'd assist her to the restroom, bathe her gently, and brush what was left of her soft, natural hair. I'd remind her how beautiful it was, hoping to lift her spirits, even if just a little. Her hair was soft to the touch, a lovely salt-and-pepper color. Then, depending on how she felt that day, I'd carefully place her wig on or wrap a scarf around her head.

It was so hard to see her like that, so different from the strong, vibrant woman I had always known. Cancer had ravaged her body, and she was fading away. As I look back now, I realize I was withering too.

Mentally and emotionally, I was slipping. At 16, I didn't know how to handle it or make sense of what was happening. It felt like I was having an out-of-body experience—watching everything unfold but unable to fully grasp it. I tried to help as much as I could, giving up things like team tryouts and time with friends, just to be by her side.

I didn't care about anything else. I just wanted to be there for her, in case she needed me. Every day at school, I would worry, thinking, What if I come home and she's gone? That thought weighed on me constantly.

When my mother slipped into a coma, I was devastated. I couldn't make sense of it. I kept thinking, 'This isn't supposed to happen. She's not supposed to be sick in the first place. She's supposed to live a long life.' By that point, hospice had become a constant presence in our home.

My mother passed away the day after my 17th birthday, on May 3, 1996—a date that is etched into my soul forever. For a long time, I carried that day with a heavy heart, seeing it as a painful reminder. She hadn't been awake for my birthday; she lay there in that hospice bed, barely holding on."

I don't remember having cake or balloons that year, and I

likely told everyone not to bother. After all, what was there to celebrate? We had just lost Mom.

The day is still a bit foggy in my memory, but I do remember going into her room, sitting beside her bed, and softly saying, Hey, Mom, it's my birthday today. I sang to her, Happy birthday to me, happy birthday to me, hoping—praying—that she would wake up, open her eyes, and say, Happy birthday, baby. But she didn't.

Looking back, I realize just how traumatic it must have been to lose my mother, especially just one day after my birthday. It's hard to fully grasp now, but I also see how much I needed her presence, even in the smallest way then. And in a strange, comforting sense, she was still there. It was almost as if she waited for just one more day. If she had passed on my birthday, I honestly think I would've been even more lost than I already was after her passing..

Her holding on for those extra days now feels like her final gift to me. I'm so thankful for that. I thank her for not leaving before or on my birthday. I truly believe God allowed her to stay just a little longer, and for that, I am forever grateful. I don't know how my heart would have handled losing her on my birthday—it might have broken me even more than it already had.

My birthday had come and gone, and the day that followed felt heavy in a way I couldn't explain. That morning, my dad knocked on my bedroom door. He opened it softly and said, "Nina, Nina, get up, baby. She's gone." I didn't say anything back—I couldn't. I went into shock. I sat up, got out of bed, and walked into her room. I saw the sheet pulled over her head.

I had still been holding onto a sliver of hope that somehow, some way, she'd pull through. But seeing her like that made everything painfully real. The rest of that day became a blur. I don't remember the ambulance coming or how they took her body out of the house.

It felt like life kept moving around me while I was frozen in time, watching it all unfold like a movie I wasn't ready to be in. My mind just couldn't handle the reality of it all, so it checked out—escaping because it was the only way I could cope.

Losing my mother wasn't the first time my siblings and I had faced grief. Before her, we had lost our grandmother on my father's side in 1993. I remember going to her funeral with the rest of our extended family. The sadness was palpable, but it hit even harder when it was time to walk toward her casket.

Seeing her there, lifeless, was almost unreal. As a child, I think part of me believed that people, especially those we love, would live forever. That moment was a shock to my young heart. It was also the first time I saw my father cry—a memory that stayed with me, because I wouldn't see him cry again until we lost my mom. I can't even begin to imagine what he was going through, bearing the grief of losing his mother and then a few years later, his wife, while still trying to stay strong for us.

We had even lost a beloved pet the year before our mother passed. At the time, Mom was away visiting my sister in Wisconsin, and I'm so glad she was able to do so before she passed.

This is a picture of my mother and sister LaShon in Ladysmith, WI, taken in 1995. By this time, my mom's hair had started to thin, and she was wearing a shorter cut.

I remember my brother and our cousin who lived across the street from us having to bury the dog in the woods. If you've ever had to say goodbye to a pet that feels like family, you understand how deeply that loss can affect you, especially as a child. My mom, as always, made sure we were all okay afterward, comforting us through sadness.

Looking back, it's interesting to me now that we went through those losses before losing her. Maybe it was God's way of preparing us, though I can't say it softened the blow for me. Still, in hindsight, it gave me some perspective on how loss shapes us—whether we're ready for it or not.

3 Through My Sister's Eyes: A Different Type of Grief

(This chapter was written by LaShon S. Smith - my beautiful, extremely smart, older sister)

On May 3rd, 1996, my phone woke me up. As I moved to answer, I already knew it was my father, and I knew why. I answered and heard my dad say, "Shon, be calm." Then he told me that my mother had passed away. He reminded me to be careful because I was pregnant. I remember sliding down the wall, holding my stomach, realizing I was about to become a mother while I had just lost my own. No words can describe that pain or the feeling of immediate personal loss.

The next few hours are still a blur, but eventually, I made the necessary phone calls to my family in Milwaukee.

Two weeks before my mother passed, I was in Fayetteville, North Carolina. I can still hear the sound of her crying aloud as I walked out the front door to return to Milwaukee. It was a cry filled with despair and complete loss. Though I didn't admit it then, I knew that was going to be the last time I saw her alive.

I was 25, having just graduated from college less than a year earlier, and now I had to mentally prepare myself to help my father and siblings make my mother's final arrangements. I needed my doctor's approval to fly, and thankfully, I was given a note to do so.

Now, picture this: a very pregnant young woman, wearing a cute beige maternity short set, trying to catch a flight out of town. My entourage included my aunts Shirley and Barbara, and my cousin Troy.

First Flight: As we boarded, the stewardess asked me how far along I was and if I was flying alone. I politely told her I had company. As I made my way to my seat, I felt a tap on my shoulder. Of course, it was the pilot. He looked at me with wide eyes and asked how far along I was. I calmly replied, "I'm 9 months pregnant, but I have a doctor's note, and I'm not due for another 2-3 weeks." As he walked away, I heard him announce, “Put your seatbelts on, we’re about to take off.” I’m pretty sure he was determined to get me off that plane as soon as possible, and we did land quickly. When we arrived in Charlotte, we were allowed to exit right after first class. There was a golf cart waiting to take us to the next terminal. I think my aunts enjoyed that ride more than I did!

Second Flight: Some passengers from the first flight were on our second flight, and they began switching seats to ensure my aunts, cousin, and I could sit together. They knew why I was flying and wanted to make sure I was comfortable. Once again, we were able to exit the plane early, right after first class. I’m sure those lovely individuals just wanted to ensure I didn’t go into labor on the plane!

My father picked us up at the airport in Fayetteville and took us to the house. That was tough—it hit me hard that my mom was really gone. Walking into her home and not seeing or hearing her broke my heart. But I had to push my emotions down and go into "big sister/oldest child" mode. It was time to get things done.

Southern hospitality is something else! The neighbors brought food for the pre-past, wake, and repast—chicken from Bojangles, store-bought meals, pasta, cakes, desserts, you name it. Since I was pregnant, they also made sure the streets were cleared in case I needed to get to the hospital.

The day of my mother’s wake was a test for what would come next: her funeral. My grandmother and aunts were "baby-ready" because I went into pre-labor during the funeral. My father, sister, grandmother, and one of my aunts took me to the hospital, but I was sent home. Before leaving, I told the nurse to keep my file close—I knew I’d be back soon. That night, my sister wasn’t allowed to leave my side per my grandmother's instructions.

The next morning, my water broke, and I went to the hospital to have my baby. I had previously asked my mother if she could name the baby. She said that if it were a girl, her name would be Carmen, and if it were a boy, Cameron. That night, at approximately 8 p.m., I gave birth to my beautiful daughter, Carmen G. Smith. My family experienced both joy and sadness. I believe my mom wanted to ensure we didn’t stay sad for too long.

The next morning was Sunday, and it just so happened to be Mother's Day. In the span of three days, I had gone into labor at my mother’s funeral (May 10th), had my first child (May 11th), and experienced my first Mother's Day (May 12th) without my mother. To be continued...

4 GROWING UP WITHOUT HER

Growing up without my mother—honestly, I don't even know where to begin. So I'll start by saying it was hard, and it sucked tremendously. My mother passed the day after my birthday, and as I mentioned before, I had just turned 17.

I was in that in-between phase of becoming a young woman, on the cusp of graduating high school a year after her passing— I was at an age when a young girl really needs her mother. I felt incomplete, like I wasn't ready for the next chapter of my life. It was like I wanted to be put back in the oven to finish cooking before moving forward.

After my mother passed and the funeral had ended, the family members who came to support us returned to their own lives, and we were left to face our new reality alone—just as they had to do. My sister LaShon later moved down to Fayetteville, NC because my senior graduation year was coming up.

We had all suffered an immense loss, whether we were her children, husband, siblings, or friends. The road ahead was going to be difficult, and we knew it would be a long time before we could find our way without her.

Eventually, we moved out of the house we had lived in with her in Fayetteville, NC.

To fill in a bit of backstory—I hadn't mentioned this earlier—we had moved to Fayetteville from Milwaukee, WI because my parents had separated. I won't go into the reasons for their separation here, as I don't have all the details and it's not relevant to this part of the story. But when my mom told my dad how sick she was, he came down to be with us, as he should have.

And just like that, everything changed. The trajectory of our lives changed forever after that point, in ways we couldn't even imagine at the time. In the months after my mother's passing, I went through so much mentally and emotionally. I was overwhelmed with sorrow, lost in a fog of depression. I didn't know how to exist without her, let alone figure out how to become a woman.

I remember one day, I was hanging outside on my dad's van—you know, one of those old 90s Chevrolet Mark III Conversion Vans. Do you remember those? I was just standing there, looking up at the sky as if I was talking to God.

And mind you, at that point in my life, I didn't really know God yet. I wasn't the girl who liked putting on dresses and stockings to go to church. But I still looked up and asked, "How am I supposed to become a woman? Who's going to help me with that?"

Looking back, I realize that I wasn't just asking who would guide me—I was asking how I was going to grow into the woman I was meant to be…a strong, successful, emotionally healthy, well-rounded woman. There was a depth to that question, and I was desperate for answers.

It felt like she was taken from us way too soon. She had four children, all of us still young—even my older sister, who was in her early twenties at the time, still needed her mother. And as my sister mentioned she was also pregnant with my niece before my mom passed? The road ahead without her was going to be tough, and in that moment, when I made that statement, "How am I supposed to become a woman? Who's going to help me with that?" I was voicing that hard reality.

When we moved, it wasn't far—just to another house in the same neighborhood. My dad decided to stay in Fayetteville, NC, and find work there. I think ultimately he didn't want to uproot our lives again and move us back to Milwaukee, especially since we had just lost our mother, and he had just lost his wife.

It was already a huge adjustment. I'm not sure if being in the same neighborhood affected me much; we were literally right around the corner from our old house. But what really started to sink in was the fact that she was truly gone.

Every moment that should have been fun during my last years of high school felt empty. I didn't have the energy or desire to commit to anything beyond just going to school and coming home. The excitement of it all was gone because a part of me wasn't there anymore, and this pain became a constant companion.

At this point in my life, the weight of losing my mom was hitting me hard. There was just too much going on—way more than I could handle mentally. I had never been into smoking, cursing, or drinking before she passed, because my parents didn't play about that kind of stuff.

But during this time, my grief started to come out in ways I wasn't proud of. Black and Mild's became my thing.

I'd sit in my room, smoking and blowing the smoke out the window so nobody could smell it. I'd light up whenever I felt sad or stressed, even when my dad was home. Whether he ever smelled it or not, I don't know, but at that point, I really didn't care.

I had no real way to deal with the pain, and my dad wasn't the type to sit down and talk about emotions. We never talked about my mom's death in a healthy way, or went to therapy?

I started being out of the house more, hanging around the wrong type of guys and becoming sexually active. I knew I wasn't living the way I was raised. Growing up, you couldn't even say "shut up" without my mom or dad giving you a serious side-eye. They didn't play that.

But there I was, turning to smoking and seeking comfort in relationships with guys, trying to cope with the pain. Yet, none of it filled the emptiness. I still missed my mom, and I longed for my dad to be more present for us. The truth was, our lives had taken a drastic turn, and we were only at the beginning of what was to come. We hadn't even begun to see the full picture yet.

Eventually, my dad started dating again. I want to say about 6 months later after our mothers passing. There were times he came home drunk, and we'd argue because I didn't like how he was acting around us. It felt like I was the parent trying to check him. Now that I'm older, I get it—he was grieving too. He had lost his wife, and maybe he was also still dealing with the pain of losing his mom.

Now, he had to raise us on his own, and in his mind, I guess he thought we needed a new mother figure. But at 17 years of age, I wasn't having it. It just felt way too soon for him to date.

By the time high school graduation was approaching, I still had no real interest in school, other than finishing my classes and going home. The last after-school activity I was passionate about was track and field. I loved the sport, but I never tried out. When my mother was very sick, it just didn't feel right to go to practice knowing she was at home, gravely ill, and might need me at any moment. So, I gave it up, and after her passing, the desire to continue just wasn't there.

But there were days when I'd still walk by the field, watching the team practice from a distance. I remember one afternoon, a classmate called out, "Hey Nina, you should come try out!" I just shook my head and said, "No, I have to go home."

Some of my friends knew my mom had been sick and had passed away, and a few of my teachers knew as well. I remember one teacher even came to my house after my mom's passing to offer her condolences and check on me. I thought that was incredibly kind, and it meant a lot to me. It wasn't something she had to do, but she took the time to show she cared. I will always appreciate her for that small, yet meaningful, gesture.

With only not even a year of high school left, it felt like a battle just to make it through. I was constantly fighting off waves of sadness and depression, trying to wrap my head around the idea of graduating without her there to see it.

The thought of walking across that stage without her cheering me on was almost unbearable. But something inside me kept pushing, reminding me, "You need to graduate." My grades slipped—I went from being an A and B student to barely holding on with C's—but I made it. I graduated.

On graduation day my dad and my siblings were all there. I remember walking across the stage, scanning the crowd for my dad. I knew he was running late, and I kept thinking, "He better be here." I wished so badly that my mom could've been there to see me.

My dad did make it, though. I didn't see or hear him during the ceremony, but after it was over, we all met up to take pictures. I was grateful that, at the very least, he was there for me in that moment.

I graduated from Seventy-First High School, home of the Falcons, class of 1997. Fast forward a bit, and in January of 1998, my dad remarried—the woman he chose to settle down with, just one year and eight months after our mother's passing.

It was another blow, but I kept my feelings to myself. When they asked me to stand as a witness, since they had married at the courthouse in Fayetteville, NC, I did what I had to do.

We ended up moving to Sumter, SC, where my father's new wife lived. I wasn't ready to call her "mom" or anything like that—I barely knew her. None of us really knew where we were headed. I had never even heard of Sumter, and honestly, I didn't want to go.

But I didn't have a choice. At that point in my life, I didn't have any solid plans except to keep working, which I'd always done. I don't remember us packing up any furniture, just our clothes. It was like we were leaving one home, still feeling the weight of my mom's passing, only to go live somewhere else again. But life was moving forward, whether I liked it or not. And so was my dad, it seemed. So, we had no choice but to make the most of whatever came next.

The way my dad handled the move wasn't the best—no big family sit-down to explain why we were moving or to check in on how we felt about it, to make sure we were okay and understood why we were moving. It was more like, "We're moving, let's get packed, and we're leaving on this date." As we drove down to Sumter, I had no clue what to think.

The only thing going through my mind was that we were moving into this woman's house, and I didn't even really know her. I mean, we had met her a few times, mostly after they got married we would hang out with her more, but she wasn't around us daily since she worked in Sumter, SC, which is 2 hours away.

As we pulled into her place, I noticed she lived in a trailer park, and I couldn't help but think, 'What is this?' There was nothing wrong with trailer parks, but it was just so different from what we were used to. It felt rural, and we were accustomed to being well-traveled and living in houses, so it was a big shift from the lifestyle we knew.

However, being military kids who moved often, I tried to keep an open mind. I stayed quiet and remained polite, thinking maybe, just maybe, things could work out. She might even become a mother figure over time. But I wasn't ready to call her 'mom' just yet.

When we got to her trailer, she told us to make ourselves at home and showed us where we could put our things. It was a two-bedroom place—one room for her and my dad, and the other room, the small one in the back, eventually became Leonard's because he was the youngest. Me and my other brother? We were stuck sleeping on the couch.

I couldn't believe it. I remember thinking, "Is this really how we're supposed to live for the rest of our youth?" Me and my brother on the couch while my dad and his wife had their privacy in a bedroom? It was hard to wrap my mind around, and honestly, it didn't feel like a real family unit at all.

For the first few months, things weren't good. My dad's wife became mean, and she didn't know how to adjust with us being in her home. She was strict and over-the-top about how clean she wanted her house. She'd fuss instead of talking to us calmly, and if my brothers didn't clean to her standards, she'd complain to me or take it up with my dad. It was frustrating.

Eventually, my brother—the one just a year younger than me—stayed with us for about four months before he decided he was leaving. He moved back to Milwaukee, WI, to live with family and finish his high school years there. After graduating, he ended up joining the Army.

One day, I came home from work, and she was fussing again because the house wasn't up to her standards. I think the dishes weren't done or something. I hadn't even been home, but she blamed me anyway, saying I should've kept my brother in line since I was the oldest.

I snapped. I told her straight up it wasn't my fault—how could it be when I hadn't even been home? For all I knew, my dad could've been the one to leave the place messy. But she didn't care. Next thing I knew, she pulled my dad aside for one of their private talks. When he came back out, he looked at me and said, "You have to leave. She wants you out."

I was stunned. I asked, "What do you mean she wants me out? Are you really going to let this happen? Are you seriously choosing her, someone you're still getting to know, over me, your daughter?"

But he didn't stand up for me. He just repeated, "You have to leave, and you have to leave now." That moment changed everything. My relationship with my dad was never the same after that. From that moment I honestly questioned what kind of relationship we even had. He raised us the best he knew how, but as far as the father-daughter bond we had once shared? It had faded greatly.

At the time, I was working at Captain D's, a seafood restaurant. I had left home, but with nowhere else to go. I ended up asking a coworker if I could stay with her for a while until I figured things out. However, that turned out to be a poor choice. I didn't like the people she associated with, and the neighborhood felt unsafe. I was angry at my dad and felt completely abandoned, but I was also 18, so I guess it was time to spread my wings and figure out life on my own.

He had completely turned my world upside down. I didn't know where to turn, but I knew I couldn't stay in that apartment with my coworker much longer. Eventually, I reconnected with an old high school friend and moved back to Fayetteville, NC. We got an apartment together, and that's when I started trying to figure out life on my own.

All these events, one after another, felt like the ripple effects of my mother's death. It was as if everything in my life was unraveling year after year in the aftermath. But let me take a step back for a moment to acknowledge a very spiritual encounter I had with God while still living with my dad and his wife.

This is important because it played a significant role in my journey and will make more sense as I continue. I remember one day, back when I was still living in the trailer with my dad, his wife, and my younger brother...

They had all gone out somewhere, but I didn't feel like joining them—I just wanted to stay home and rest. So, I was sitting there flipping through the channels when I stumbled upon a pastor on TV. I can't remember who he was or what exactly he was talking about, but every word he spoke hit me deep. It was exactly what I needed to hear in that moment as if God was talking only to me.

By the end of his message, I found myself saying the prayer of salvation, right there in the living room, and giving my life to Christ. Afterward, I felt an overwhelming sense of peace come over me. I couldn't fully explain it, and I didn't completely understand everything that had just happened, but I knew I had experienced a real encounter with God. It was a moment I'll never forget.

I wanted to mention this piece because again, it's such an important part of my journey. That moment of finding peace in the midst of everything falling apart was a turning point for me. It's when I started to understand that, even in the hardest times, I wasn't alone. God was there with me.

Eventually, living with my friend didn't work out, and neither did a relationship with a guy I was dating at the time. I found myself in a tough spot, unable to find work right away. My friend, always full of ideas, suggested we both work at a strip club. Hesitant, I agreed.

I'm not sure what I was thinking at the time, but the club

was far from glamorous. They hired both of us, and I remember working just one day. I couldn't get comfortable with the skimpy bikini I had to wear or the idea of dancing in front of strangers. To make things worse, we were behind cage-like stages, which felt even more dehumanizing.

What really sealed the deal for me—and I can laugh about it now—was when it was my turn to dance. An old man came in, sat right in front of me, and flipped a penny at me. In that moment, reality hit me hard. I was better than this. I realized what I was doing and knew this was the end of my short-lived stripping journey, lol.

I found work elsewhere and started working two jobs just to cover my half of the rent, but I knew I wanted more for my life than where I was at that moment—college, a better future, something. I didn't quite know what it was yet, but I always had this feeling that there was more out there for me.

I worked at the Waffle House close by and at Hardee's, balancing both jobs for a while to save up money so I could leave Fayetteville, NC. Things were getting chaotic, and my roommate, along with some of the people she was hanging out with, just weren't a good fit for me anymore.

I had been saving my tips with plans to move, but someone—though I'm not sure who—ended up stealing the money I had hidden. I was furious, but it only reinforced that it was time for me to go.

At this point, my dad and stepmom had been trying to reach out, asking me to come back. But after how things had ended, I didn't trust that they were being sincere. So, I turned to my sister and asked if I could stay with her in Milwaukee. She said yes, so I moved there, with the mindset of this is going to be a fresh start.

Milwaukee, WI was a breath of fresh air. It gave me the opportunity to spread my wings, reconnect with relatives I hadn't seen in years, and spend time with my sister. Before leaving North Carolina, I had made the decision to disconnect from the past and start anew, this time with a clear goal in mind: I wanted to work was the plan, get my own place, and go to school.

Life in the Midwest was different, and there was an adjustment period, but I was genuinely happy to be there. From riding the city bus to experiencing the cold winters all over again and getting familiar with the local personalities, everything was new.

I remember my first solo adventure catching the bus downtown one day to take care of something in the city. With my semi-Southern roots still in full swing (mind you, we were military children), I walked through the streets greeting everyone I passed with a friendly "hello," just as I would have in North Carolina or South Carolina.

To my surprise, no one responded. I thought to myself, "What's wrong with these people?" When I arrived back home and told my sister what had happened, she gently reminded me, "You're not in the Carolinas anymore." It was a small moment, but it was a clear reminder that I was in a new place, with its own distinct culture and way of life.

This is a picture of my sister on the left, my niece Carmen (named after our mother), and me during the time I lived with my sister for a few years, either in 1999 or 2000.

Did my whole life change in this new place? No. Despite my hopes for a fresh start, life was still complicated. Not long into my journey, the ex-boyfriend I had ended things with reached out, and we got back together for a short while. I considered giving him another chance—after all, we had been together for over a year, and he was familiar to me. He even flew up to Milwaukee to spend time with me.

But eventually, I realized we were worlds apart. I was evolving into a different woman, no longer the same young girl he once knew.

I began to refocus on working and applying for school, but the absence of my mother weighed heavily on me, especially as I tried to figure out who I was and what I wanted to do with my life. People I encountered would tell me, "You could be this," or "You should do that," but nothing seemed to stick. It felt like I was wandering through life blind, just rolling the dice and hoping I made the right choice.

I truly needed my mother at this point in my life. I

needed her guidance, especially when it came to figuring out relationships, dating, and navigating adulthood. I longed to call her and share my breakups, to laugh with her over funny stories about guys or just to hear her advice.

But I didn't have that—none of us did. My siblings and I were left to process life without her, and my father wasn't available either. It felt like I was navigating everything alone. My sister was there, but she, too, was trying to find her way, becoming the woman she wanted to be without our mother's guidance.

My sister was renting an apartment at my aunt and uncle's place, and by that time, I had been living with her for almost a year. One day, my aunt asked if I wanted to go to church with her. I figured, why not? It couldn't hurt, so I agreed and said, 'Yes, I'll go with you.

When we arrived at the church, the experience felt different. I hadn't been to church in a long time, and although it was unfamiliar, it was unlike anything I'd experienced before. The atmosphere was powerful, and I later found out that the pastor was actually my aunt's nephew, making him my cousin.

His message was incredibly moving, his wife and all the other people there were so warm and welcoming. I can't recall if it was that day or shortly after, but I found myself going back. Months later, during one of the services, when they called for anyone who wanted to give their life to Christ, I walked up to the altar and prayed the prayer of salvation, surrendering my life to the Lord Jesus Christ that day.

I felt that same peace I had experienced that day alone in the trailer. But this time, the change felt real and lasting. The difference from when I had prayed with the pastor on TV was that this felt like something I was truly drawn to even more than before, something necessary at this stage of my life. It was as if God was guiding me to a deeper, more connected walk with Him. I now had an example of what being part of a church community looked like, with people I had come to trust, and I wanted to experience that for myself.

It wasn't just about going through the motions anymore; I had a desire to attend church and feel the connection and renewal I had glimpsed during those first few visits. This time, I truly felt transformed spiritually, like a light had been turned on inside me, and the darkness was lifted. It's hard to put into words, but it was a life-changing experience.

This new experience would shape me in ways I couldn't have anticipated. There's too much to tell in detail, so I'll sum this part up. A few months after giving my life to Christ, I felt a new life transition was unfolding. God was moving me from one life to an entirely new one, both spiritually and naturally.

The scripture in Ephesians 4:22 says, "You were taught, with regard to your former way of life, to put off your old self, which is being corrupted by its deceitful desires," and in this essence, I knew that my spiritual transformation needed to be reflected in my physical life as well.

I decided to move out of my sister's house and into the home of a woman from my church who became like a spiritual mother to me during that season of my life. She not only welcomed me into her home but embraced me as part of her family, and for that, I'll always be deeply grateful. There's much more to that story, but I'll save it for another book.

The transformation I was going through felt strange—there's

really no better way to describe it. After giving my life to Christ at the altar that day, everything felt different when I returned home. My surroundings, my environment—it was almost as if I didn't recognize where I was anymore. Something significant had shifted inside me.

The church I attended was called Higher Heights Ministries, which later became Spoken Word. It was my first home church. Growing up, our family wasn't raised in the church. We spoke of God, sure, but regular churchgoing wasn't part of our routine.

My mom was raised Catholic, and my dad was Baptist. Occasionally, we'd attend church on special holidays like Christmas or Easter, and when we stayed near my grandparents, we'd go with them a time or two.

But we weren't the kind of family that attended church every Sunday, went to Sunday school, or lived a life fully dedicated to Christ. So this was all very new to me—new in every sense of the word, a fresh experience that was reshaping me in ways I'd never imagined.

5 MISUNDERSTOOD GRIEF

Misunderstood grief—what does that mean? Let me explain so you can fully grasp this part of the story. Grief is something we all go through at some point in life, but what many don't realize is that it doesn't always look the way we expect it to.

It's not just about the loss of a loved one, although that's often what we associate it with. Grief can manifest in so many ways: the loss of a relationship, the loss of a job, the loss of a dream or future we had imagined for ourselves. It's that deep sense of sadness and emptiness that sometimes doesn't make sense to others, and often, it doesn't make sense to us either.

Misunderstood grief happens when people around us—or even ourselves—don't fully grasp the weight of what we're going through. Maybe they expect us to "move on" quickly or "get over it" just because it doesn't look like traditional grief.

They may see us smiling, going to work, or continuing on with life, and assume that everything is fine. But inside, we might be struggling with feelings of confusion, loneliness, or even guilt, because we're still carrying that grief, even if it's not visible to the outside world.

In this chapter, I will use my own personal journey to walk you through misunderstood grief. Grief shows up in many different forms and is often misunderstood by others—and sometimes even by ourselves. For me, grief manifested in a variety of ways throughout my life.

It wasn't just about the loss of my mother, but also the loss of, dreams and planned futures, and even pieces of myself. It showed up in my struggles with family dynamics, feeling displaced and disconnected, and in my difficulty trusting others. Grief crept into my work, my relationships, and even the way I viewed my future.

It's crucial to understand that grief isn't a linear process. It doesn't simply fade away after a set period of time or after meeting certain expectations. Grief is a journey, and each of us experiences it in our own unique way.

I want you to realize that it's okay to grieve in your own way, at your own pace. You don't have to conform to anyone else's idea of what grief should look like. Your grief is valid.

Okay, now let's reflect on all that I have shared with you so far to understand how this form of grief showed up in my life...

First, after my mother's death, I turned to smoking and relationships as a way to cope with the pain. To outsiders, it may have seemed like typical teenage rebellion or just bad decisions, but what many didn't realize was that these behaviors were driven by my grief. The loss left such a deep void in my life, and smoking and seeking comfort in relationships were my ways of filling that emptiness.

I also began to withdraw from school. I had no real desire

to engage with my classes or activities. The only thing I cared about was finishing school and going home. The track and field team, a sport I had loved, was something I gave up entirely. I lost my passion, not because I didn't care anymore, but because grief took away the energy I had for anything outside of my immediate reality.

Another way grief surfaced was through the anger and sense of abandonment I felt toward my father when he remarried. Although my relationship with his new wife eventually improved after returning to South Carolina, at the time, it wasn't just the new marriage that hurt me—it felt like I was losing him too. I had already lost my mother, and now it seemed as though my dad was starting over without considering us. That anger stemmed from the unresolved pain of losing my mother and feeling like I was being left to navigate life on my own.

When I moved out of my dad's home and lived with unsafe people in difficult environments, many might have seen it as poor decision-making. But for me, it was a reflection of how lost I felt. I was trying to find stability in a life that felt completely turned upside down, grappling with grief while trying to survive emotionally and financially.

Graduation was another moment where grief quietly made its presence known. As I approached this milestone, I felt unfinished, like I wasn't ready for adulthood without my mother's guidance. It's something a lot of people might not understand, but I was mourning the fact that I wouldn't have her there to help me through that important chapter of my life.

When my father asked me to stand as a witness at his courthouse wedding, I did what I had to do. I didn't express my hurt or confusion at the time, and I just went along with what was happening. To others, it might have looked like I was fine with everything, but internally, I was struggling with grief.

That silent endurance was yet another form of misunderstood grief.

Later, my decision to become a stripper might have seemed reckless or desperate to those who knew me, but this too was an expression of grief. I was trying to gain control over a life that felt chaotic and uncertain. I was working multiple jobs to make rent and survive, but I knew deep down that I wanted more for my future—college, stability, and purpose. Grief clouded my judgment and led me down paths I wouldn't have otherwise taken.

Throughout this time, I kept a lot of my feelings to myself. Whether it was about my mother's death or my father's remarriage, I bottled up my emotions, not wanting to express the pain I was carrying. To the outside world, it may have looked like I was holding it together or being strong, but internally, I was deeply struggling. This emotional withdrawal was another way grief showed up in my life.

After my mother passed, it felt like my life began to unravel. One thing after another seemed to go wrong, and it all felt like the ripple effects of her death. To others, it might have seemed like bad luck or poor decision-making, but grief was at the heart of it all. My life felt like it was spinning out of control because I was still processing the enormous loss I had experienced.

Finally, when I found faith and returned to church, it wasn't just a spiritual awakening—it was also part of my grieving process. I was searching for meaning, comfort, and healing in the midst of everything I had gone through. This was a form of grief too, trying to find a way to deal with the pain through faith. While it may have looked like a positive life change, it was also a way for me to heal from all the loss and turmoil I had experienced.

Each of these experiences was grief showing up in different, often misunderstood, ways. Grief doesn't always look the way we expect it to—it can manifest in behaviors, choices...and emotions that others might not recognize as mourning, sometimes leading us into not-so-good places in life, but also, on the flip side, guiding us toward a positive direction.

There's a beautiful scripture, Psalm 30:11, that says, "You turned my mourning into dancing; you removed my sackcloth and clothed me with joy."

Grief can be a heavy and painful journey, often leading us through some of life's darkest moments. Yet, with time, it holds the promise of healing, transformation, and the gentle restoration of joy.

Even in our deepest sorrow, there is hope that, God can turn our mourning into something beautiful.

6 CARRYING ON

Carrying on wasn't easy, but it was necessary. Over the years, my relationship with my dad continued to fade, but eventually, we regained good ground.

It was crucial for me to continue healing, reconnecting, and mending broken relationships. I had to do this—not just for my own well-being, but I knew that the steps I took towards my own healing journey could also have a positive impact on my siblings.

My mom wouldn't want me to stay stuck in a place of mourning forever. That's not living. My twenties came and went, and now my thirties were here, staring me down. And I had to go on, even though it wasn't easy. It still isn't.

I still have moments of reflection. There are times I wish she was here. There are times when I get upset, and sometimes, the little things still trigger me—especially being around other people or during the holidays.

But here's what I hold on to: a cute little way I know she's still with me, outside of her blood running through me. I mean, her DNA is literally a part of mine! Lol. But there's one memory I keep close to my heart, and it's the one that always reminds me that she's still with me.

Before she passed, we had this moment—just the girls. It was in my mom's bedroom, and my grandmother, my mom, and I think my sister was there also. My grandmother asked us to hold out our hands, and when we did, we all noticed something wild: our hands looked exactly alike. All of us, with the same hands. My grandmother kept saying, "Look, look at our hands! We all have the same hands!"

Now, that moment, I don't take for granted. I believe it was meant to be a memory etched in my soul forever. So every time I get sad, and I miss my mom—I'm a big baby, mind you, I used to sit in her lap all the way up to age 15, that's how much I loved her—whenever the overwhelming sadness tries to take me, I think of our hands. It's like a little reminder that she's still here, in the things we shared, in the things that will always bind us.

Fast forward I had joined the Army. Around my 6th or 7th year in the Army, I started getting this nagging feeling that it was time to move on. But move on to what? I had no clue, yet that feeling kept popping up every now and then.

I had just been stationed in South Korea, Camp Red Cloud (Uijeongbu) to be exact, for a one-year assignment. I got there, in-processed, learned my job, & started getting settled. I even took extra college classes and military courses to stack up training I thought would benefit me as a leader. But still, that feeling came back: "It's time to get out."

I started questioning it. Why now were these thought popping up? I had plans—plans for my career, plans for what assignments I wanted next, and the career track I was aiming for. But that feeling just got stronger. So, I began to pray, to really talk to God about it. The first question I asked was, "Lord, what is my purpose? What am I supposed to be doing with my life? Is there something else I'm meant to do?"

I was really asking, "Well, if it's not the Army, God, then what is it?" The weight of getting out kept getting heavier and heavier. That feeling wouldn't let go, no matter how much I tried to focus on my Army plans that thought just kept coming back. So one night, I prayed again...

I prayed, "God, if it's meant for me to get out of the Army, if that's what You want me to do, then station me in Columbia, SC." At the time, Columbia was where my dad, his wife, and my brother Leonard had moved.

They had relocated from Sumter, SC, to Columbia, because my dad had taken a job at the VA hospital, and if I was going to be stationed anywhere, I wanted to be closer to family.

My previous assignments were far from family with the exception of an uncle I have that lives in Colorado—Dugway, Utah was my first duty station (which, by the way, most people don't even know exists—I sure didn't when I first got orders), Aberdeen, Maryland & then South Korea. So yeah, being near family felt right.

This photo was taken during the Color Guard ceremony at the Battalion Ball for the Air Defense Artillery (ADA) at Aberdeen Proving Ground.

After that prayer, the overwhelming urge to leave the Army lightened for a while. I focused on work, school and took extra military training when I could, the Army's combative program was one of my favorites and, as usual, I also started planning my next career move. In the military, you can't get too comfortable—you've got to stay sharp.

I didn't like the idea of staying in the same rank for too long, especially once I felt I had outgrown it. For example, I started as a Private First Class, but staying in that position for five years felt unnecessary, so I worked hard to earn each subsequent rank and promotion.

I would sit down with my leadership to talk about my options, my Sergeant Major suggested Drill Sergeant school. I figured, why not? I hadn't heard anything definitive from God telling me to leave, so I applied for Drill Sergeant school, knowing it would come with an extension on my contract if I got in.

Well, let me tell you—not only did I get accepted into Drill Sergeant school, but it was located in none other than Columbia, SC, at Fort Jackson.

When I say I had no idea where the Drill Sergeant Academy was or even thought much about it, I mean it. I just saw it as one of my options for a broadening assignment, like becoming a recruiter or an instructor. That was as far as my thought process went, honestly it was too many other things going on at the time!

So, I completed my tour in Korea, took a small break, and then reported to the Basic Training Unit where I would shadow until my start date with the academy. Fast forward to just before my graduation, and guess what? I received my assignment orders and I was staying on as a Drill Sergeant at Fort Jackson, right there in Columbia, SC. Can you believe I didn't make the connection right away?

I was like, 'Okay, Lord, you were serious about me getting out.' But it didn't fully register that this was God answering my prayer.

I was too caught up in the excitement of the position and quickly got busy working—working hard, like a 'Hebrew slave,' as they say, ha-ha. I even got promoted to the next rank while I was a Drill Sergeant. My focus was so much on advancing that I completely forgot about the prayer and that nudge I had felt to move on.

This photo was taken during the "White Phase" of Basic Combat Training (BCT) with the 2-60th Battalion at Fort Jackson, while I was instructing a trainee in marksmanship training.

Years were flying by, and then COVID hit. At this point in my career, I was working at the in-processing unit on FT Jackson, where we prepped what the Army calls "trainees" before sending them off to Basic Training.

Even with the pandemic shaking up the world, we were still working, still taking in Soldiers. It was such an uncertain time for everyone. And wouldn't you know it— even with all that was going on here comes that feeling again, the same one I'd had back in Korea. It was heavier than ever, but I tried to reason it out, convincing myself it was just stress from the situation.

So, I did what I thought would help—I called my

mentor, trying to get some reason. I even talked to my dad, who helped calm me down a bit, though he definitely didn't want me to leave the Army. My mentor gave me sound advice, telling me to really think it through, make sure I was sure, and to have a solid plan if I did decide to get out.

As the world started to adjust to the new normal, COVID was slowly clearing up, and I remembered my previous plans of putting in a Warrant Officer packet. Now seemed like the time to move forward with that.

So, I submitted my application, took the required physical, and passed. Shortly after, I got an email saying, "Congratulations, you've been accepted to attend the Warrant Officer Course (WOC)."

I was on my way to Warrant Officer School!

It felt like things were finally coming together, but life has a way of throwing unexpected challenges our way. Even as I was moving forward with my career, I stayed in close contact with my family.

I have to say that I'm so thankful my dad and I were able to restore our relationship before things took a turn. It wasn't perfect, but we were working towards something better. He was there for one or two of my promotions, and he even pinned me for one of them.

He also attended my course graduations (ALC & SLC) and came to one of my award ceremonies. I will forever cherish those memories.

In this photo, my dad had the honor of pinning me when I was promoted to the rank of Staff Sergeant (SSG).

This photo was taken during an award ceremony while I was working at the In-processing Battalion at Fort Jackson.

Well, at least that was the plan—to keep building those moments. But then, life threw a curveball—my dad got sick. COVID was still in full swing, and the world was under mask mandates and safety precautions. It was a tough time, and nothing about it was easy to navigate.

At first, it was just me taking my dad to his doctor's appointments when he couldn't drive himself. Then things took a turn for the worse.

7 MY FATHER’S SILENT STRENGTH

Let me first share a bit more about my wonderful father. My father's name was James Harvey Smith Jr., born in Dayton, Ohio, on June 24, 1950, to Ina Mae Quinn and James Harvey Smith Sr.

Growing up, I knew my father as a kind man, always eager to hold a conversation. He definitely had the gift of gab—he could talk to a stranger for hours without missing a beat.

My father was a proud military veteran, serving an impressive 26 years in the United States Army. He began his career, as I learned from his DD 214, as an 11C—an Infantry Indirect Fire Crewman, commonly known as a mortarman. Later, he transitioned to a 92G, a Culinary Specialist, responsible for food service operations and ensuring Soldiers were well-fed.

This was the role we were most familiar with as a family. We have so many fond memories of going to his dining hall as kids—eating, spending time together, and just being there while he worked. The dining hall became a special place where, even though he had to work, we could still connect as a family during the holidays.

Because of my father's career, our family moved around a lot, but the two places I remember most clearly, because we lived there the longest, are Germany and Fayetteville, North Carolina. Moving frequently was just part of military life, and my father's dedication to his service shaped not only who he was but who we were as a family.

My dad deployed a lot, and if you know anything about the military, you know the toll deployments can take on the individual and their family. My mom held it down while he was away. We would always send him care packages with baked goods to remind him of home.

I remember one particular deployment—before he left, he was strong, healthy, and full of his usual energy. But when he came back, he was so thin. He didn't look like the dad I was used to seeing, and it really hit me how much those deployments could be wearing him down.

In short, my dad was a good man, and he fathered us the best way he knew how. He wasn't one to get overly emotional or expressive about his feelings. I don't remember having deep conversations with him, and I don't recall ever seeing him cry—except at funerals. He wasn't the type to wear his emotions on his sleeve, but he was loving in his own way.

He was protective, and like any typical father-daughter relationship, we had our share of moments when we butted heads. He could get on my nerves, but he was my dad—the man partly responsible for giving me life in partnership with my mother and God, lol. Despite our differences at times, he was always there in his own way, providing and protecting, as fathers do.

I could write an entire book about my father, and maybe one day I will. But for now, I'll leave you with that brief summary and move on to how I saw him handle my mother's death.

Despite their separation before she passed, he still stepped up, coming down to help take care of her and fulfill his responsibilities as a father to us. That moment, even after all they had been through, showed the depth of his character.

During the time my mother was sick, my father came down after being notified of just how serious her condition was. I remember him being around, helping out here and there, all the way until she passed. Though my memory is a little foggy on the details from back then, I never saw him break down.

My dad just wasn't that type. I'm not saying he didn't cry as he watched his wife—despite their personal relationship issues—wither away. It had to tear him up inside. After all, they had been married for over 20 years and had known each other since well before high school. Sometimes I would imagine what they were like before children came along—just two people who had grown up together. Who were they, just James, or 'Ponnie' as his siblings called him, and Carmen, or 'Carol' as her siblings called her?

Through my mom's passing, my dad stayed what I thought was strong. But after she was really gone, it started to sink in. A couple of times, he came home drunk, and we would get into it. I'd ask him, "What are you doing?" because he'd be out late, worrying me, wondering where he was. So, he'd catch it from me when he finally got home.

But looking back, I realize that was his way of releasing his grief in the only way he knew how. When I'd ask if he was okay, I'd get what I call the auto-response: 'Yeah, don't worry about me, Nina. I'm fine.'

It wasn't until much later, after receiving further education, training, and gaining insight from my military experience, that I began to understand that my father was likely dealing with his emotions in the way that felt most familiar to him—by holding them in.

In an interview with Therapy for Black Girls, Dr. Thema Bryant shared:

"There is often a stigma within the Black community, and particularly for Black men, when it comes to being emotionally open. Many Black men are taught from a young age that showing emotions is a sign of weakness or vulnerability, and that to be a 'real man' means to be strong, stoic, and self-sufficient. But this emotional suppression is harmful—it prevents them from healing, growing, and forming deep, authentic connections."

I believe this was a combination of how my father was raised and his military career. His idea of strength was holding everything inside when things were emotionally hard to express, and that's how I believe he navigated parts of his life, even during his deepest moments of grief.

So was his silence really strength? At the time, I believed he kept his real emotions to himself because he thought it was the best thing to do. But looking back, I wonder: if only he knew how much we needed to see him cry, to break down—heck, even hit a wall—something, anything that showed us he was feeling the same pain we were. His silence left us unsure of how to navigate our own emotions, and as the man we looked to for guidance, he unknowingly set the tone for how we all handled that grief.

We needed to know it was okay to hurt, to release our emotions. But instead, my dad stayed quiet, carrying on with life as if nothing had changed. In his silence, we all followed suit—just going through the motions, not truly acknowledging that our mother was gone.

I can only speak for myself, but I know I mirrored his way of mourning—internalizing everything and shutting down. As Dr. Thema Bryant observed, that kind of silence is harmful. It stifled our ability to heal, grow, and build deeper, authentic connections with each other and with others.

Instead of uniting in our grief, it felt like we drifted apart, scattered by the weight of our own pain. That emotional silence hung over us for years like a fog we couldn't shake—and in some ways, it still lingers to this day.

I'm not sure if my father ever truly spoke about my mother's passing—or even his own mother's death—to a therapist or someone in a related field. If he did, he never mentioned it. I can only hope that, at some point, he found a way to unburden himself fully, to share what he was carrying with someone who could offer the empathy and care I knew he needed.

When he eventually remarried, the woman he chose, though not an immediate fit for us at first, turned out to be exactly what he needed. I watched him change for her—opening up in ways I had never seen before. She was a talker, and she got him to talk, too. He started to express himself in ways that were completely new to me. As life went on, and we all grew older, moving out (or kicked out in my case) to build our own lives and careers (except my younger brother), my dad found real companionship in her.

She even got him going to church again, y'all! But honestly, she ended up being good for him, and it showed.

8 LOSING HIM TOO

I remember one night he called me, saying he needed to go to the ER. I rushed to pick him up and took him to Lexington Medical Hospital late that night. The nurses, let me tell you, had no bedside manner whatsoever. They really pissed me off with their attitude, and I had to bite my tongue to keep from snapping because I didn't want to stress my dad out.

He was already uncomfortable. They were running tests, checking his kidneys and other things, but no one really explained what was going on, just that his kidney levels were high. One doctor mentioned it wasn't good, but that's about all the information we got.

Honestly, their care was lacking. You'd think people in their position would treat patients and families better, but I guess if it were one of their own loved ones, they'd have acted differently.

We sat there for hours. Leonard was in the waiting room, and I stayed with my dad in the hospital room. I brought my school books with me because I knew it would be a long night. But honestly, I didn't think too much of it. My dad was always so resilient, so strong-looking. He didn't even look sick that night, which made me think everything was going to be okay.

Then, out of nowhere, while we were waiting for a nurse to come back, my dad looked at me and said, "Nina, it's y'all's time now." He repeated it again, "It's y'all's time now." I let it sit for a second, then brushed it off and said, "Okay, Dad, stop talking like that. You're going to be fine." Shortly after, the nurse came in, and they discharged him.

I had no idea how sick my dad really was. He never told me the full extent of his health issues. That night, I took him and Leonard back home, made sure they were settled, and told them to call me if they needed anything. The next day, I went right back to work, thinking everything was going to get back to normal.

Over the following weeks, my schedule was crazy. Between taking my dad to his doctor's appointments and working a 24-hour staff duty shift, I barely had time to breathe. I'd come home, shower, knock out some homework for my bachelor's degree, and crash into bed, just trying to keep everything afloat.

I need to quickly recap and fast forward through this part because it's still a lot for me to process. As I mentioned, on November 1st, I took my dad to the ER. A week later, on November 8th, he fell in the bathroom and hit his head on the tub. And then, before we knew it, November 15, 2020 arrived—a day that would forever change me and my siblings.

I remember taking him and my brother to the store to grocery shop and run errands that week, and I think I even took my dad to another doctor's appointment as well. But when it comes to what happened on the 15th, I had to ask my sister for the details and the exact date. It seems crazy, right? Because I was the one physically there with my dad and younger brother, while my sister was all the way in Milwaukee, yet I still have to call her to remember certain things.

That's the thing about "grief fog"—it's like this mental haze that makes it hard to remember certain things after you've experienced a deep loss. It's almost like your brain's trying to protect you by blurring out parts of reality, but it also leaves you feeling disoriented, like you're piecing together a puzzle with some of the pieces missing. So, as much as I try to remember, there are some parts I just can't clearly hold onto.

I was completely spent that week from work and everything else going on. I remember choosing to rest on the couch in the living room on the 15th—my body was just done. My brother later mentioned that he had tried calling me that afternoon after realizing that my dad wouldn't wake up.

The strange thing is, I didn't hear the phone ring at all, so I hadn't answered. I was in this deep, almost foggy sleep, and at some point, I vaguely remember hearing my phone, but it was like I was stuck in a sleep stupor, like this heavy weight was keeping me down on the couch, preventing me from waking up.

Eventually, I managed to wake up, saw the missed calls from my brother, and I called him back right away. "Leonard, what's wrong?" I asked. He said, "It's Dad. He won't wake up." My heart sank. I rushed over to my dad's house, went straight to where he was, and when I saw him lying there unresponsive, I immediately told my brother to call 911. Then, I started performing CPR.

(Let's pause here.)

Apologies, I needed a moment before continuing. I performed CPR on him until the paramedics arrived, which was pretty quick. When they assessed him, they pronounced him DOA—dead on arrival. They told us he had been gone for quite some time.

As they started doing what they needed to do, we stepped outside to answer questions from the other paramedics. And then, as they were talking to me and my brother, they rolled my dad's body past us.

Jesus, is this really happening? I felt myself go into shock mode and take-charge mode at the same time. I was the one who had to make the call to my siblings to tell them... Dad had just passed away.

This is exactly the moment in life where I should have been screaming in rage, but I kept it all inside for now. I thought, 'You've got to be kidding me.' Were we in trouble or something? What in the world was happening that me and my siblings deserved this second blow? I could feel it coming, slowly—this one was going to knock the wind out of me.

Moving forward, we started planning for his funeral. My other siblings and two of my nieces came down. It was still during COVID, so none of his brothers, who were still living, or other from his side of family could make it, nor could anyone from my mom's side who knew him well. My father and stepmother were separated at the time (long story), so her involvement was very minimal.

All the planning, including the costs, fell on us because, for some reason, my father didn't have life insurance. You can imagine how upset I was that we had to cover the expenses for his funeral. It was hard enough, but to make matters worse, Thanksgiving was just around the corner—another holiday spent grieving, and this time, grieving both of our parents.

I will say my stepsister did help when it came time to clear out his apartment. We decided to have our father cremated. The day of the funeral arrives, and again, the whole process was overwhelming.

His step wife didn't attend, and there was still limited communication with her, even though they had been married for over 15 years. My stepsister and her family were extremely late—like, "the funeral's over" kind of late. You talk about adding fuel to a fire already burning with frustration… listen.

The funeral itself was nice and peaceful, though. My dad was a veteran, so they did the 21-gun salute. Every time those shots fired, it ripped at my very soul. Each shot was a painful reminder that he was really gone. My brother and I are also veterans, but we didn't wear our uniforms.

I think we just wanted to be his children in that moment, if that makes sense. I don't remember shedding many tears at the funeral or any at all; I was still numb, just trying to be strong for everyone else. I've come to understand that I go into this emotional state as a defense mechanism, probably because of my experience with my mother's passing.

After the service, my siblings and nieces all stayed at my house. The boys took my younger brother's room, my nieces took mine, and my sister and I slept on the couches. During this time, my two dogs—an American Staffordshire Terrier and a Maltese mix—slept all over the place. I think they were taking turns comforting all of us, each in their own way. My brother had to leave early, but before anyone else left, I wanted to make sure we captured the moment together with a family photo.

Although two of my nieces and a nephew couldn't make it down to South Carolina due to work commitments and weren't in the photo, it was still a beautiful and cherished moment. We stood there, feeling the weight of everything we had been through, yet also the love and connection that held us together.

A family photo taken just before they headed back.

I had to snap a photo with my two fur babies—Crystal on the right and Candy on the left.

The time eventually came for my sister, brother, and nieces to leave and head back to Milwaukee, WI, and soon I'd have to return to work. Now, it was just my younger brother and me. I play a bit of a caretaker role with him—he deals with schizophrenia and bipolar disorder, though he's incredibly smart. Our journey together was just beginning, and I wanted to make sure we were going to be okay.

While my family was still here, I didn't cry. I didn't shed many tears at all during the funerals for either of my parents. I felt like I needed to keep my emotions in check, holding back as we made all the arrangements and got everything together.

It's like I have this natural mute button for my emotions when it comes to situations like this. I don't know. But when everyone left, that's when I went into a deep, sad place of mourning.

The bed became my best friend. There were days I would just cry—screaming cries into my pillow, trying to muffle the sound because I didn't want to concern my brother. He was grieving too, and that big-sister part of me didn't want him to see me like that. I knew I needed help processing this loss because it felt like a punch to the gut. I kept having these overwhelming thoughts: "I can't believe both of our parents are gone." I felt like an adult orphan.

I promised myself that since I hadn't processed my mother's death in a healthy way, I was going to approach things differently this time. I started therapy, which helped a little, but I quickly realized that although my therapist's credentials listed grief counseling, her style just didn't resonate with me. She often went off topic, which distracted from the healing process. I ended up doing most of the talking, and while she was kind and offered a listening ear, it wasn't exactly what I needed.

The focus wasn't really on my father's loss, which is where I needed the most support. Here's a tip: make sure your therapist specializes in exactly what you need, and if it doesn't feel like a good fit—don't hesitate to find someone else. I left the sessions with so many unprocessed emotions that I still needed to work through.

Even though I was working on completing my bachelor's in psychology at the time, which gave me some insight into the psychological aspects of grief and loss, I still needed both professional and spiritual support. This was a time when I knew I had to lean on God more than ever, while also figuring out how to release and process all that I was feeling about my father's passing.

I mean, how was I supposed to juggle all these emotions, return to work like everything was fine, make sure my brother was okay, and continue pushing through school so I could graduate? That last part felt all too familiar—once again, I was working through pain to ensure I graduated, only this time, it was from college.

Some months had passed, and we entered a new year without my dad, still grieving and trying to navigate life without him. In the midst of it all, I graduated from Liberty University with a Bachelor of Science in Psychology: Christian Counseling. I knew I had to attend my graduation—I needed to. Life had thrown its punches, but this was a milestone I was determined to reach. As excited as I was, I knew the day would be bittersweet. My father wouldn't be there, and the painful truth hit me—now, neither of my parents would get to see me graduate from college.

Still, I packed everyone up—my brother, and my two fur babies—and we hit the road. I drove nearly five hours, only stopping for gas, and we barely made it in time. I told Leonard to find a seat while we left the dogs at the hotel, and I ran down to the field, quickly found my chair, and sat down. I glanced around, hoping to see Leonard, but when I couldn't spot him, it brought me back to my high school graduation, scanning the crowd for my dad and wishing my mom could've been there.

I quickly refocused as they asked us all to stand. When my name was called, I smiled big. I was proud of myself, yet sad at the same time. But I'm so thankful that my brother was there to see me walk across that stage and help with the fur babies during the trip. That meant the world to me.

College graduation - Liberty University, July 2021

College graduation - Liberty University, July 2021

During this time, my little fur baby, Candy, had gotten sick. She made it to my graduation, but when we returned home, she took a turn for the worse. I had been taking her back and forth to the vet before the trip, as she was struggling with kidney issues. She stopped holding down food and was losing a lot of weight. The vet told me she didn't have much time left and I had to make a difficult decision: either continue letting her live in pain or have her put to sleep. I held off as long as I could, but I eventually realized that keeping her around was only causing her more suffering. It broke my heart to see her like that.

Crystal, my other dog, was always by Candy's side—cuddling her on the bed, the couch, or wherever Candy went.

Candy on the left and Crystal on the right.

Crystal on the left and Candy on the right.

Candy had reached a point where I had to administer IV fluids at home to keep her hydrated. I think I was just holding on to her because it was too soon after my father's passing, and I wasn't ready to let go again. But eventually, I made the decision to have her put to sleep.

That drive was long and painful. I held her in her blanket, loving on her as much as I could during those final moments. I had never had to put a pet to sleep before, and it was devastating. Saying goodbye was harder than I could've imagined. I dropped her off wrapped in her blanket, said my tearful goodbyes, and drove home with tears streaming down my face. It was hard to believe I had to let go of someone I loved so soon after losing my dad.

Looking back, I don't even know how I made it through that season. All I know is that God must have been watching over me closely. I came home heartbroken, and for the next few months, I felt deeply sad and depressed. I went through the motions—going to work, coming home, and just lying around the house.

One day, Crystal let out this deep, mournful howl. I was downstairs at the time and rushed upstairs to her, but I knew what it was. She was grieving too, in her own way, releasing her sadness for Candy. You see, Candy had practically raised Crystal.

I got Crystal as a puppy, and Candy had stepped up, nurturing her like a mother. Their bond was special, and losing Candy was hard on both of us.

Despite having a good career and feeling solid in the education I'd gained, I still found myself needing support in ways I hadn't expected. Grief has a way of making you realize that no matter how successful or grounded you feel, there are moments when you simply can't carry the weight on your own.

One thing about me is that I'm naturally the type of person who encourages others, always pushing people to be their best and go after more. I'm the one people come to for a listening ear or advice. But when life hits you hard, when it's your turn to face the storm—who do you turn to?

Let me tell you, that can be difficult when you're the person everyone turns to for strength. But it's part of my calling, and I wouldn't trade it. Still, during that time, I found myself on my knees in prayer more times than I can count. Thank God for my personal relationship with the Lord Jesus Christ; He became my anchor through all the pain and confusion.

But even with faith, I knew I needed support from those around me. So, I reached out to people I trusted with my emotions. Having the right community is crucial, especially when you're grieving the loss of loved ones. You need people who will sit with you in your pain, who can offer empathy, love, and understanding.

It's okay to stay friends with people who don't have that natural capacity for empathy, but when you're grieving, you need to be selective about who you allow into your emotional space. It's not about their character—it's just about who's equipped to help you in that moment.

As time passed, I continued to grieve the loss of my father and my fur baby Candy while shouldering the weight of life's responsibilities—working, paying bills, and helping my brother adjust to his new life with me, our new life together. At the same time, I faced a major decision: should I stay in the Army or leave? Was all this life pushing me forward the answer to a prayer I had prayed long ago?

My initial plan was to stay in, especially now that I had the added responsibility of caring for my brother. I ignored the recurring thought that maybe it was indeed time to leave the Army, from that prayer I had prayed years ago.

I kept considering that time when I asked God, "If I'm supposed to get out of the Army, station me in South Carolina." And that's exactly what happened. But instead of recognizing this as a possible sign, I stayed focused on my goal of remaining in the Army, especially since I had been accepted to Warrant Officer School.

The next step was to add my brother as a dependent so he could travel with me. I submitted all the necessary paperwork, reached out to the right departments, and even sought help from my supervisors, who did everything they could to assist. Despite all my efforts, the process hit a wall. His medical documentation from his psychiatrist wasn't enough for the Army's requirements—they told me I needed to claim him as mentally incapacitated for it to be approved.

That was the final straw. I couldn't do that.

I wasn't willing to define my brother in that way, even though the truth is, the Army wanted me to claim him as mentally incapacitated. To help you understand, being classified as mentally incapacitated means that someone is considered unable to manage their own personal affairs or make important decisions due to mental or cognitive challenges.

This label could affect things like their legal rights, independence, or ability to engage in everyday activities without assistance. It's a heavy term that implies the person would need ongoing supervision or support in most areas of their life.

But that wasn't the case with my brother. Yes, he has mental health conditions like schizophrenia and bipolar disorder, but he's an incredibly smart man with personal goals. He just needs a little bit of help. Labeling him as mentally incapacitated would have felt like stripping away his autonomy, and I knew that would have impacted his life in ways that weren't necessary.

He's capable of making decisions for himself, setting and pursuing goals, and living a meaningful life. I couldn't let this label define him, because it wasn't who he is at his core. So, even if it meant sacrificing my own career, that was a choice I was willing to now make. And honestly, I feel like this was a God thing, too. It felt like God was guiding me out of the Army, gently nudging me toward the next season of my life. It was as if He was saying, 'In this season, it's time for you to move on. And since you're not quite picking up on what I've been trying to show you, ha-ha, this is how I'll help you make the transition.

So, I did just that. I declined my orders to Warrant Officer School, submitted a hardship extension to remain at Fort Jackson, and transferred to another unit on the post. This unit would carry me through to the end of my Army contract, which was set for December 11, 2023.

Why am I sharing this part of my life in the chapter titled "Losing Him Too"? I want you, the reader, to understand the significant life events I was navigating—on top of everything else—while still grieving. At times, it felt like there wasn't even space to fully process my loss.

There were moments when I had to stop and check in with myself, to breathe, to ensure I was truly living and not just going through the motions. And throughout all of this, I was still dealing with unprofessional work environments at my last unit in the Army, helping others process their painful journeys (I'll go into more detail about toxic work environments in another book, so stay tuned), making sure my brother was good, and still finding time—because I felt led—to naturally encourage others.

That's just who I am friend—a natural encourager. I have always been this way.

You want to talk about a final year in the military being heavy and stressful—sometimes unnecessarily so, due to the actions of others. Jesus, I look back now and laugh, because I truly feel like God, in those painful moments of transition, was making it crystal clear that it was time for me to leave. Just in case I had any thoughts of re-enlisting, it was a loud and clear 'No, ma'am' from above!

God had bigger plans for me, a greater assignment—one that I had no idea about yet.

Amid all the chaos, there was one bright light that helped shift the heaviness—eventually, we decided to adopt another dog. A two-month-old puppy from the Humane Society caught my attention. He was the only one lying there, covered by his sister pups, looking like he needed rescuing. I knew at that moment I had to sign the paperwork and bring him home.

When I opened the door to my house, he darted in like he had been there all along, making himself at home immediately. I picked him up and took him over to my brother, not revealing his name yet, and asked him to name him, saying he could be his pup.

My brother paused and said, "What about Ronald?" I chuckled, responding, "Ronald?!" But then I realized that was the name on his adoption papers. Well, technically, his name was Ronnie, but "Ronald" just felt too close.

For me, it felt like a little sign from God, as if He was saying, "I'm here with you all." Ronnie quickly became a perfect fit for our family. He bonded with Crystal, and she became like a mother to him. They're now the best of buds, always by each other's side.

I thought I was rescuing Ronnie, but in reality, he rescued us. He brought so much joy and comfort during those tough times, a distraction from our pain, and a reminder that even in the darkest moments, there's still light and love to be found.

Crystal and Ronnie a few months after bringing him home.

If you're grieving the loss of a loved one, I encourage you to reflect on your own journey and recognize the distractions that may prevent you from mourning in a healthy way. It's also important to find positive "distractions" that bring you peace and joy. Losing my father felt like a double blow for me and my siblings. For me, those distractions often took the form of work and added responsibilities—not in an extremely negative way, but in a way that I knew I needed to pay close attention to. I had to be careful not to get so consumed by life's demands that I forgot to process each stage of grief I was still facing, and to ensure I was doing so in a healthy way.

I had to make time to pause, breathe, and check in with myself to ensure I was okay before checking on anyone else. I want to encourage you to do the same—it's necessary to take that time for yourself. Make it a regular practice to check in with you.

My sister and I have both said it feels like we've become "adult orphans." We had to bury our parents far too soon, and that kind of loss stays with you. We all knew, deep down, that one day our parents would pass, but the hope is always that it will be when they've lived long enough to see us and their grandchildren grow and thrive.

We often imagine our loved ones growing old together and passing peacefully, but that wasn't our story. The way we lost them, and the timing, will forever be etched in our hearts. My hope is that we continue to honor them through who we are and who we are becoming—that we make them proud in this way.

I hope that all they endured and sacrificed for us wasn't in vain, that we didn't waste our lives, but instead strive to become the best versions of ourselves. I pray that we continue to live, laugh, love, and receive love in ways we deserve, cherishing the life we have and honoring their memory.

9 UNDERSTANDING GRIEF AS AN ADULT

As I've grown older and more mature, more educated my perspective on grief has evolved. The way I choose to show up and acknowledge it today is quite different from when I was younger. I've learned to embrace grief in a healthier, more intentional way. But before I dive into how that shift happened, let me first expound a little more on what I know grief really is.

Grief can often seem like a scary, overwhelming term that many of us shy away from. We tend to avoid talking about it in-depth or even acknowledging it, hoping it will fade if we don't give it attention. However, grief doesn't work like that, and it's crucial that we deal with it in a healthy way.

At its core, grief is a deep sorrow, usually in response to losing someone we loved greatly or losing something significantly important in our lives. Grief isn't just about death. It can also surface when we experience other forms of loss—like the end of a relationship, the loss of a job, or even significant life changes.

Grief shows up in many ways, and it can trigger a wide range of emotions—sadness, anger, confusion, guilt, even relief. It's important to understand that none of these emotions are wrong. They are part of the grieving process.

One thing to remember is that grief isn't a straightforward process—it doesn't follow a neat, predictable path. Instead of being linear, grief is more like a winding road that takes unexpected turns.

Sometimes, you may think you've reached a place of peace, only to be hit with a wave of sorrow out of nowhere. That's okay—it's normal. There's no set timeline for grief, and no right or wrong way to feel.

Let's talk about how grief shows up in us emotionally:

Shock and Denial – You might initially feel numb or disconnected from the reality of the loss. This is your mind's way of protecting you from the immediate weight of the pain.

Anger – As the reality of the situation sets in, you might feel angry at yourself, the situation, or even the person you lost. It can feel unjust or unfair, and that anger is a natural emotional response.

Sadness and Depression – Deep sorrow often follows anger. You may feel intense sadness, loneliness, or even a sense of hopelessness. This is a critical stage where it's essential to allow yourself to feel without suppressing the emotion.

Guilt – Sometimes, we experience guilt, feeling like we could have done something differently or wondering if we missed the chance to say or do something. It's important to remember that these feelings, while common, aren't always based in reality.

Acceptance – Acceptance doesn't mean you no longer feel pain. It simply means that you've begun to find a way to live with the loss and integrate it into your life.

Grief can take us by surprise, and it doesn't move in a straight line from one emotion to the next. Some days, you might feel at peace, and the next, a wave of sadness hits. The key is to allow yourself to feel each emotion and to honor your process without judgment.

We often hear people talk about "moving on" from grief, but I prefer the term "moving forward." You don't forget the loss or the person, but you do learn how to live again while carrying that memory with you. Mourning is an active process—it's not about passively waiting for the pain to go away. We need to actively work through our emotions, talk about them, reflect on them, and seek support when needed.

In this chapter, I want to explore not just what grief is, but how we as adults can navigate it in a healthier way. We need to create space in our lives for grief, to give ourselves permission to feel and to mourn openly. And just as important, we need to support each other in our grieving processes, recognizing that every person's journey through grief will look different.

As you read about my grief journey, you'll notice how I showed up in different seasons of my life was vastly different from one to the next. After doing a lot of soul work—through therapy, prayer, learning about myself, and diving deeper into what grief really is and how to navigate it—I've found that the weight of losing my parents has become a little easier to carry over time. That's not to say the loss isn't still profound, but how I respond now is very different from how I did when my mother passed.

When my mom died, I went through every emotion I mentioned earlier—shock, denial, anger, sadness—but I stayed in that shock and denial for a long time. I kept living as if everything was fine, but inside, I was far from okay.

The reality that she was gone, that this was our new life—me and my siblings without her—was too heavy for me to accept right away. It took time, and a lot of internal work, to even begin processing it.

Now, I've come to understand that grief for both of my parents will always be with me. There will always be moments when I'm hit with a wave of emotion because I miss them so deeply. And I've learned that it's okay to feel that. If I need to cry, I cry. If I need to scream, I scream. And if I need to lay in bed, wrapped in blankets because it feels like the closest thing to a hug, I give myself permission to do that too. This is my process, and there's nothing wrong with it.

I once heard someone say that grieving the death of a loved one is the greatest form of love you can give them, because it shows how deeply they meant to you. I believe that to be true. I can't visit my father down the street or go back in time to be with my mother, but their memories are precious gifts I carry with me every day.

As an adult, I still have my moments—and I will continue to. There are things and places that still trigger memories of my dad's passing, and there's a lingering guilt from not being able to get to him sooner. Those feelings don't just disappear, and that's okay. You can't just "move on" from something as monumental as losing your parents. Telling someone to "move on" isn't helpful—it's dismissive of the loss and dismissive of the person who's mourning.

Instead, we move forward. We take delicate, necessary steps each day, honoring our grief in a way that feels right for us. That's what I try to do, day by day, as God allows me to wake up and live another day.

Honoring your grieving process and embracing it with a "this is my journey" mindset is something I've found to be crucial. It matters because you are the one walking through it. You are the one who knows how it felt to endure what you've been through.

You understand the emotions that hit you when those waves come crashing in. I had to treat myself with extra care at times—pay attention to who I was around, monitor my behaviors, and check in with myself regularly. I also had to learn to be vulnerable with myself. By that, I mean acknowledging when I was struggling, something I wasn't always comfortable with.

This was a significant step for me because my father wasn't one to express his emotions openly, and I picked up that habit. It's something I've had to work on—and am still working on—in various areas of my life.

Grieving my father pushed me to be more vulnerable, to open up, to seek help, and to ensure I was surrounding myself with the right people. Now, at 45, I reflect more deeply on how I want to show up in life. I strive to be more emotionally healthy, which is part of my journey toward becoming a therapist. I've come to understand that life doesn't spare anyone.

I once heard someone say, "You don't reach old age without going through some things." That's so true. We all face hard things in life—things we never expected, things that hurt, and one day, we'll all know grief in some form.

But I thank God that I have Him to lean on, a source of strength that can only come through my relationship with the Lord Jesus Christ. Without Him, I could have lost my mind long ago. But if I can share for just a moment—God is a keeper.

I know Him in that way. He has shown up for me in ways I could never have imagined. I've come to realize my life is not my own. I didn't create myself, so I must acknowledge that yes, I've gone through some incredibly hard things, yes, my parents are no longer here and I miss them deeply, but God is good. He has been so good to me and my family.

10 THE JOURNEY TO HEALING

Oh my gosh, where do I begin? My healing journey, like anyone else's, wasn't a straight line—though that would have been nice. I used to wish there was some emotional graduation process for grief. Like, "Okay, she's taking the 'anger' course this semester. All that's left is 'depression,' guilt,' and passing the final exam on understanding loss.

After that, she's ready to graduate, no need to revisit these courses again." But my process was more like stumbling through a maze, hoping I was heading in the right direction. Some days, I felt like I'd made progress, and other days, it felt like I was right back where I started, completely unsure of what was happening inside me.

I had setbacks, breakthroughs, breakdowns and lessons I didn't even know I needed to learn. There were moments when all I could do was let out the loudest scream or cry into a pillow. Grief hit me hard, and I experienced different versions of it with each parent's passing.

When my father died, it compounded everything—bringing me back to the loss of my mother, and now the loss of both parents. If my grief had a word, it would be a loud, resounding "NOOOOO!" Punches, kicks, and screams were definitely called for during this grief appointment I never scheduled. Yet somehow, I had to prepare myself to move forward, to start a new healing journey that reopened old wounds I didn't even realize were still there.

On my hardest days—and there were plenty—I would think back to when my dad was in the hospital. He kept telling me, "It's y'all's time now." At first, I didn't fully grasp what he meant, but over time, I realized he knew he was getting ready to leave this earth. In that simple phrase, I found comfort.

To me, "It's y'all's time now" meant, "I've lived my life, and it's time for you all to start living yours." He was passing the torch, and in that encouragement, I found strength to continue my journey toward healing.

His words gave me a little push, even though I had those moments where I was like, "But God, this isn't fair. I don't want to live this life without my parents." And to be clear, it wasn't about being suicidal—I was just angry at times, frustrated that we all had to endure this kind of pain. I'd find myself asking, "What's the lesson in all this, God?

Because I don't get it." Yet, even in those moments of deep frustration and confusion, I chose to move forward day by day, moment by moment. I made the choice to feel it all, to talk it through, and to have those tough, honest conversations with myself—and with God, pouring out my heart in those "God, I need You to hear me" moments.

Healing is truly a journey, one that takes time, patience, and, most importantly, surrender. It's not easy. There's no quick fix or shortcut through grief, but it can be a powerful, transformative process when we allow ourselves to release into it fully. Whether you're grieving the loss of a loved one or any significant loss in life, allowing yourself to go through the process is key.

Here are a few steps that helped me, and I hope they'll help you along your journey:

1) **Acknowledge Your Pain**: Don't try to suppress or ignore it. Grief is real, and it deserves space to be felt. It's okay to cry, scream, or be upset—it's part of healing.

2) **Talk About It**: Whether it's with a friend you can trust with your process, therapist, or even journaling, express your feelings. Keeping things bottled up only adds to the emotional weight you're carrying.

3) **Take it Day by Day**: Grief comes in waves. Some days will be harder than others, and that's okay. Focus on getting through each moment as it comes, without putting pressure on yourself to feel "better" right away.

4) **Lean on Your Faith**: If you're a person of faith, lean into that. For me, my faith was a lifeline during those dark times. Turning to God, even in my anger and confusion, gave me peace and hope.

5) **Create Space for Healing**: Sometimes, healing means giving yourself permission to take a break from responsibilities and focus on your emotional well-being. Whether that's through meditation, prayer, or simply taking a quiet walk, find ways to create space to heal.

6) **Find Comfort in Scripture**: I found reassurance in God's word during times when I felt alone, especially in Matthew 28:20, which says, 'And surely I am with you always, to the very end of the age.' This scripture comforts me, reminding me that even in the darkest moments of my grief, I am never truly alone. God is always with me, and He is with you, too.

7) **Remember Healing is a Journey**—a journey that can bring you closer to yourself, to God, and even to the loved ones you've lost as you carry their memory forward. It's hard, yes, but it's also a process that, when fully embraced, can bring peace, strength, and even growth. Remember, God is always there, walking with you every step of the way, and you will find your way through.

I wish I could tell you how wonderful the path to healing is, but the truth is, healing isn't a smooth ride. It's not always pretty, and it's definitely not easy. There will be days when it feels like nothing is changing, like you're stuck in a loop of pain and frustration. But even on those days, you're moving forward in ways you may not see yet.

The grief doesn't go away overnight, and you won't have all the answers, but you will find a way through it. It's okay to not have everything figured out. What matters is that you keep showing up, for yourself, for your loved ones, and for the life that's still waiting for you. God is right there with you, every messy, difficult step of the way.

11 Offering My Story

I've hesitated to share my story for a long time. I didn't want to revisit those deep parts of my life that I rarely speak about, reopening old wounds and reliving the pain all over again. And that's exactly what happened when I started writing this book—the memories came flooding back, and so did the tears, along with the lingering grief still within me.

But in the end, I realized that sharing isn't just for me—it's to help others. Someone out there may be going through something similar or even worse. My journey through grief, loss, and healing has been full of challenges, setbacks, breakdowns, and unexpected lessons.

There is something so therapeutic about telling your truth. Talking about what you've gone through, because the first person it frees, before you free anyone else, is yourself. I've learned that in many ways, our healing isn't just a personal matter, it's a shared experience.

Each of us walks a unique path, but we can often find comfort, strength, and insight in the stories of those who have walked before us. It's my hope that by offering a bit of my own story, I can help guide you, inspire you, and remind you that you're not alone in your journey.

My intention here isn't to make my story the focal point, but to use it as a way to illustrate that healing is possible. It's important for you to know that I've been where you are now—lost, confused, angry, or even numb. I understand what it feels like to wake up every day with a heavy heart and to question how life will ever feel normal again.

The road through grief isn't a straight one, and it's certainly not easy, but it is one we don't have to walk alone. By sharing the raw and real parts of my story, I hope to encourage others to embrace their own healing journey with grace and patience.

I'm sharing this part of my life because I believe there's power in vulnerability. By opening up about my losses, my struggles, and the steps I've taken to heal, I hope to provide a bit of guidance to anyone who might feel stuck or overwhelmed.

Healing doesn't have to look perfect, and it doesn't have to be quick. But with the right support, it is possible. If you find yourself in need of help as you walk through your grief, I invite you to reach out to me for grief coaching.

You can visit my website at **www.thatdoseofencouragement.com** to learn more about my services.

If for any reason I'm not the right fit for you, I also maintain a list of mental health professionals who may better suit your needs. Remember, you don't have to walk this journey alone—there is help available, and you deserve to find the peace and healing you're searching for.

Thank you for taking the time to read Grief Looked Like Me. I hope that by sharing a portion of my grief, it has helped you in some way. If it has, feel free to send me an email and let me know how it has impacted you.

I would love to hear from you. Please email me at **MinninaSmith@thatdoseofencouragement.com.**

Captured Memories

Mom and my sister LaShon

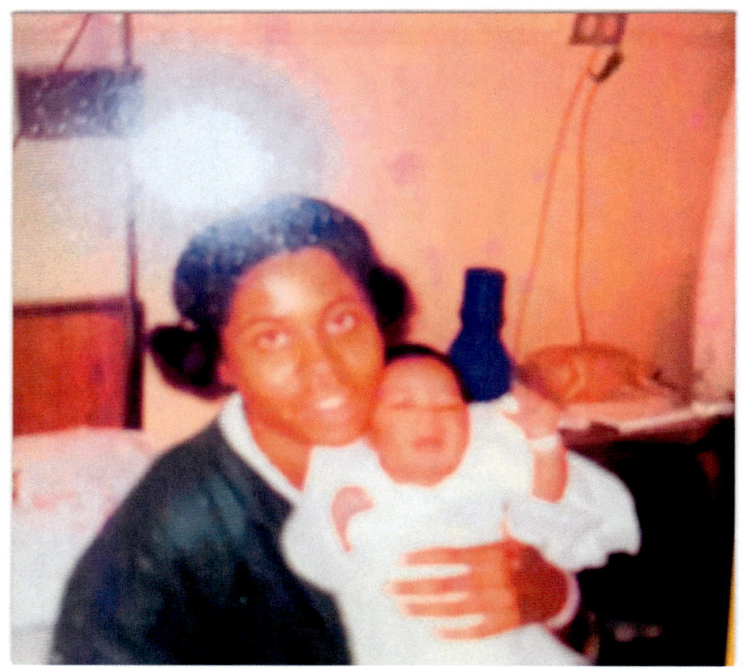

Mom and I

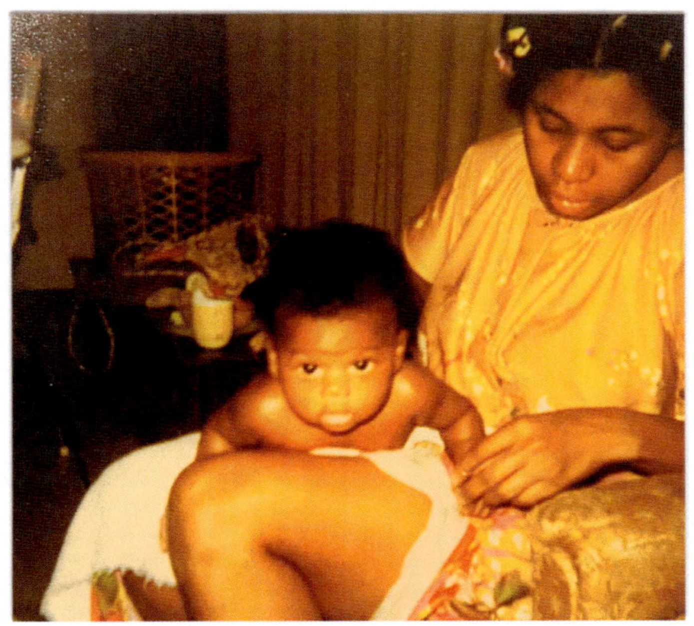

Mom and my brother James

Our youngest brother doesn't have any remaining baby pictures, but here's a photo of him now.

Family photo taken before our youngest brother was born.

Mom, LaShon and I

My brother James and I during Christmas when we lived in Germany.

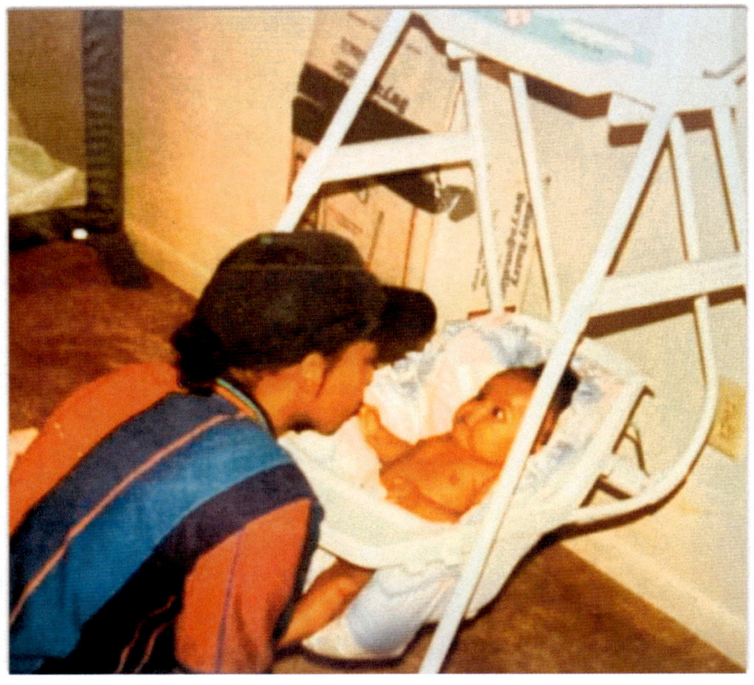

Here's a photo of me playing with my niece before heading off to my shift at Hardee's.

The grandchildren of James and Carmen - my sister's children

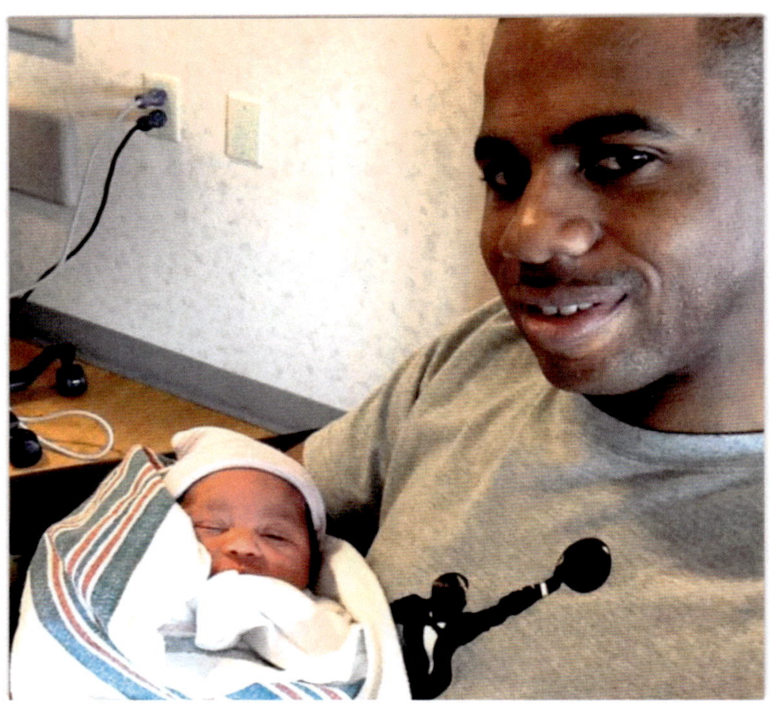

Another wonderful grandchild of James and Carmen—
my brother's daughter. She has grown up so much and
is much older now.

Here's Candy, my first fur baby, at our old apartment when she was healthy.

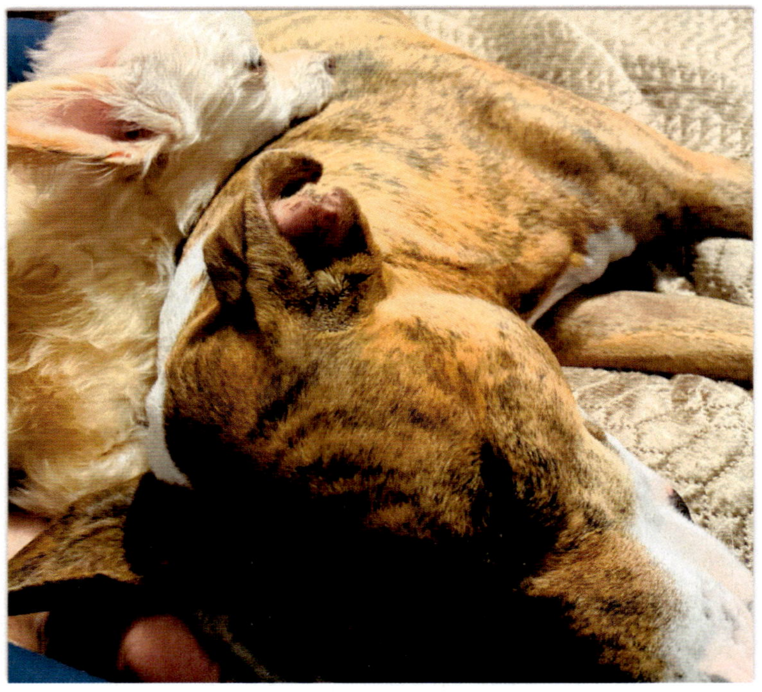

Here's Candy and Crystal. As Candy's health declined, Crystal became her comforting companion

Siblings for life. We're a special team, now and forever!

ABOUT THE AUTHOR

Minnina Smith is a life coach, mentor, military veteran, author, daughter, sister, friend, and dog mom to two spoiled fur babies. She is also a graduate student pursuing an MS Dual Degree in Clinical Mental Health and School Counseling with a focus on Marriage and Family Therapy (MFT)). She is deeply committed to helping others navigate their journeys of grief, personal development, and purpose empowerment.

Through her life coaching service, That Dose of Encouragement, Nina has dedicated herself to guiding individuals through life's challenges, offering them the tools and support needed to heal and thrive. In the future, she plans to extend her services to include professional counseling as well. Nina's experiences, including the loss of both parents, military service, and her dedication to education, have uniquely positioned her to connect with people on a personal level. She understands the complexities of grief and life transitions and uses her own story as a foundation to inspire and encourage others. Whether through her writing, coaching, or speaking engagements, Nina creates a space where others can find clarity, hope, and purpose.

This is Nina's second book, and she envisions many more to come. Her work is driven by a desire to inspire readers to embrace their own paths, trust the process of healing, and pursue their purpose with confidence. Her mission is to empower people to live fully, even in the face of loss, and to help them find strength and purpose in their journeys. To connect with Minnina M. Smith and learn more about her coaching services, visit **www.thatdoseofencouragement.com**. You can also tune in to her **From Grief To Purpose Podcast** on **YouTube @fromgrieftopurpose** and follow her on Instagram and Facebook **@minninasmith.**

Made in the USA
Middletown, DE
30 January 2025